LIFE WORKS!

LET'S PULL TOGETHER

HOW TO WORK IN TEAMS

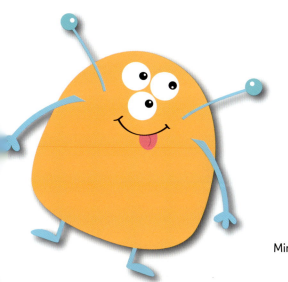

by Rachel Rose

BEARPORT PUBLISHING

Minneapolis, Minnesota

Credits: cover background, © cammep/Shutterstock, cover 1, 4, 5, 8–9, 11, 13 15–17, 19–20, 22–23 (monsters) © world of vector/Shuterstock; 2–3, 12–19, 24 (background) fishStok/Shutterstock; 4 (box) © Abscent/Shutterstock; 4–6, 8–11, 20–23 (background) Pogorelova Olga/Shutterstock; 6, 21 (bubble) © Erta/Shutterstock; 6 Gelpi/Shutterstock; 7L, 22–23 © Rawpixel.com/Shutterstock; 7R © Serhii Bobyk/Shutterstock; 7B © Monkey Business Images/Shutterstock; 9–10, 14, 18, 20 (signs) © olllikeballoon/Shutterstock; 12, 17 © ESB Professional/Shutterstock; 16T© fizkes/Shutterstock; 16B ©JR-50/Shutterstock.

Library of Congress Cataloging-in-Publication Data

Names: Rose, Rachel, 1968- author.
Title: Let's pull together : how to work in teams / by Rachel Rose.
Description: Minneapolis, Minnesota : Bearport Publishing Company, 2022. | Series: Life works! | Includes index.
Identifiers: LCCN 2021030917 (print) | LCCN 2021030918 (ebook) | ISBN 9781636914275 (library binding) | ISBN 9781636914329 (paperback) | ISBN 9781636914374 (ebook)
Subjects: LCSH: Teams in the workplace--Juvenile literature. | Cooperativeness in children--Juvenile literature. | Small groups--Juvenile literature.
Classification: LCC HD66 R654 2022 (print) | LCC HD66 (ebook) | DDC 302.3/5--dc23
LC record available at https://lccn.loc.gov/2021030917
LC ebook record available at https://lccn.loc.gov/2021030918

Copyright © 2022 Bearport Publishing Company. All rights reserved. No part of this publication may be reproduced in whole or in part, stored in any retrieval system, or transmitted in any form or by any means, electronic, mechanical, photocopying, recording, or otherwise, without written permission from the publisher.

For more information, write to Bearport Publishing, 5357 Penn Avenue South, Minneapolis, MN 55419. Printed in the United States of America.

CONTENTS

Teamwork 4
Teams All Around 6
New Teammates, New Friends 8
Better Together 10
Count on We 12
Trust Your Teammate 14
Listen Up! 16
Story Time 18
A Good Leader 20
A Little Help 22
Glossary 24
Index 24

TEAMWORK

Sometimes, we can do things by ourselves. But other things are hard to do alone. We need help.

Working together makes it easier to get things done. And it can be fun. When we work together, it's called teamwork!

TEAMS ALL AROUND

Teams are everywhere. Sometimes, we pick a team to join. Other times, we are put on a team to solve a problem.

Think of teams you have been a part of. Make a list of teams at school, at home, in clubs, and more!

A family team can clean much faster.

Classmates team up on a school project.

We can score a goal on a soccer team.

7

NEW TEAMMATES, NEW FRIENDS

We can be on teams with friends we know. But sometimes there are people we don't know on our teams.

BETTER TOGETHER

How can teams work better? By learning more about other people, we learn more about the team!

TRY IT: WE'RE THE SAME

1. Find a buddy. You may not know this person yet!
2. Take turns sharing things about yourselves.
3. Go back and forth until you find three things that you have in common.

COUNT ON WE

All of us are good at some things. And we need help with others. That's where a team can come in handy!

A person who is good at drawing and a person who is good at writing would make a great team for a poster!

On a team, we can each use our **strengths**. We can count on others to do the things we need help with, too.

TRUST YOUR TEAMMATE

When we count on others, we need to **trust** them. Practice working as a team while using trust!

TRY IT: TRUST TALK AND WALK

1. Team up with a buddy. Clear some room in your space.

2. Pick a start and stop point. Choose a speaker and a walker.

3. Go to the start point. If you are the walker, close your eyes.

4. If you are the speaker, give the walker **directions** on how to get to the stop point.

5. When the walker gets to the stop point, it's time to switch!

We can **earn** trust on our team by taking care of others.

LISTEN UP!

A team is better when we all have a chance to speak and be heard. Try to be a good listener!

A good listener looks at the person who is speaking.

Paying attention to a speaker shows **respect**.

Good listeners wait their turn before they speak.

When we listen to others, often they will listen to us, too.

STORY TIME

Can listening help make a story? Work together and have fun!

TRY IT: TEAM STORY

1. Choose someone on your team to start telling a story with one sentence.

2. Have the next person add a sentence to the story.

3. Keep going so each team member adds to the story one sentence at a time.

4. Practice good listening skills so your story makes sense.

A GOOD LEADER

Some teams need a **leader**. This person is in charge. On a team, we often get to take turns being the leader.

Pick the three things that you think are most important to be a good leader.

Why did you pick these things?

A LITTLE HELP

Big things can be hard to do on our own. But sometimes all it takes is a little help.

GLOSSARY

directions instructions on how to get somewhere

earn to get something for work done

leader someone in charge of a group

respect a feeling that someone or something is good and important

strengths the things people are best at

trust to believe in someone or something

INDEX

friends 8
help 4–5, 12–13, 18, 22
leader 20–21
listen 16–18, 21
respect 16
strengths 13
teamwork 5
trust 14–15